Creating School-Community-Business Partnerships

by
Barbara J. Hopkins
and
Frederick C. Wendel

Library of Congress Catalog Card Number 97-69149
ISBN 0-87367-623-8
Copyright © 1997 by the Phi Delta Kappa Educational Foundation
Bloomington, Indiana

This fastback is sponsored by the
National College of Education Chapter
of Phi Delta Kappa, which made
a generous contribution toward
publication costs.

Table of Contents

Introduction

School-community-business partnerships are not new. The concept is to keep the "public" in public education and to involve the community in raising the child. As schools grew and more and larger schools were built, schools' ties with communities changed. Now there is a need in many communities to reconnect schools to community entities, including businesses.

Successful schools are mirrors of a successful community. And one way to ensure that schools are successful is to engage the community in the schooling endeavor. Partnerships have evolved into coalitions of administrators, business personnel, community members, classroom educators, chief executive officers (CEOs) of local businesses, parents, and students — all of whom work to enhance education and build stronger communities together.

This fastback is designed to serve as a guide to partnership program development. We begin with a brief history of partnerships, track the development of partnership programs, outline key roles, and identify the indicators of partnership program success. These indicators have been identified through qualitative and quantitative research methods — based on good common sense.

Readers should find this fastback to be a valuable starting point for initiating school-community-business partnerships in their community.

A Short History of School-Community Partnerships

Prior to the 1960s, schools had been actively engaged with the community in providing vocational education and career education. During the 1960s and 1970s, large metropolitan areas set out to develop partnership programs. One of the most common forms of partnerships at that time was the Adopt-a-School program. Other forms of partnerships included volunteers in the schools, speakers' bureaus, school foundations, homework hotlines, and mentoring programs. These programs became the foundation for the school-community-business partnerships of the 1980s and 1990s.

In the 1980s the private sector renewed its interest in public schools. Renewed participation was welcomed by some but a cause of concern to others. The fears were that business personnel would not understand school functions, that business personnel would criticize the methods and techniques of educators, that vocational education would be the only focus, and that partnerships would encroach on the professional image of educators. The "Adopt-a-School" notion of earlier days portrayed business as the dominant force in school-business programs.

However, others saw this renewed interest in partnerships as offering an important support for education in general and for specific schools, teachers, and programs. Still others saw promise in the political alliance that might be built between community power structures and the community's schools.

In 1983 President Ronald Reagan established the Private Sector Initiatives program, which provided federal dollars to support school-business partnerships. The succeeding Bush Administration followed with a goal to double the amount of participation by business and industry in education under First Lady Barbara Bush's leadership as national chair of the school-community-business partnership movement.

National symposia were sponsored through the Private Sector Initiatives program from 1984 to 1988. In 1988 the Adopt-a-School programs and school volunteer programs (in particular, the National School Volunteer Program) united with the National Partners in Education Symposium sponsors to establish the National Association of Partners in Education (NAPE). This new organization was to represent the schools and educators, businesses, community groups, and individual volunteers who worked together to enhance the education of children and youth.

Another organization evolved in 1986. Partnership directors attending the symposium felt a need to have a professional organization and network, similar to the professional organizations for elementary principals, secondary principals, superintendents, school business officials, and so on. Thus the Association of School Business Partnership Directors (ASBPD) was created to aid in the professional development of individuals in charge of directing partnership programs. In 1987 this organization affiliated with NAPE and became the Partnership Directors Network (PDN).

Partnerships of the 1980s and thus far in the 1990s have become a way for people from the community and schools to communicate valuable information, share resources, solve problems, and implement solutions. The current stage of development has been viewed by many observers and participants as the time to focus on systemic change. Others, however, have expressed concern that a focus on systemic change and America 2000/Goals 2000 has been too political. Additional concerns are that the funding and staffing for partnerships are not adequate for the task of reforming education.

Fortunately, ties to the White House and political support have remained strong, even as the national leadership has changed. President Reagan's Private Sector Initiatives evolved into America 2000 under President George Bush. Under the leadership of President Bill Clinton, America 2000 has become Goals 2000, which continues to promote community support of education with a focus on reform. Partnerships also are a key component of the school-to-work initiative.

Partnerships continue to evolve throughout the nation. With that evolution has come an identification of key indicators of partnership program success. The 1990s have been a time of increased accountability and evaluation. Productively, the national thrust includes a new phase and funding for school-to-work and school-to-careers programs, which we will explore in the following sections.

The Development of Partnership Programs

Dale Mann was a pioneer in research on business participation in public schools. In his initial study of urban programs in 1983 three-fourths of the urban districts had partnership programs, but only one-fourth of those had partnership directors or support offices to sustain partnership programs (Mann 1984). In 1987 Mann expanded his study to include smaller cities and surveyed superintendents, teacher organization representatives, school board members, business representatives, and community agency employees. Outside of the big cities, two-thirds of the superintendents said that the business involvement was really no different from what schools and civic groups had always done with schools.

Four hallmarks of "true" or genuinely reciprocal partnerships were identified:

- a coordinating structure
- multiple purposes
- multiple players
- stability

Only 17% of the partnership programs Mann surveyed had all four features of "true" partnerships.

The Growth of Partnerships

The National Center for Education Statistics (NCES) documented partnership growth from 42,200 in the 1983-84 school year to 140,800 in the 1987-88 school year. The NCES report (1989) differed from Mann's studies in that it did not include traditional involvement of parent organizations or business involvement with vocational education programs. In this study, small businesses were found to be the greatest supporter of school partnerships because so many more small business owners had a loyalty to public schools and their community. High poverty schools were more likely to have partnerships, which was explained by the conclusion that the needs were so high that businesses felt they had to help.

In the NCES study the types of partnerships were identified. Partners with the schools were businesses (54%), civic and service organizations (17%), and post-secondary institutions (9%). The other 20% was not identified by type. School staff members initiated partnerships 80% of the time. School staff members reported that their primary goals for partnerships were to foster cooperation (35%), provide incentives for students (25%), and obtain equipment (11%).

The two most frequent types of support reported by schools with partnerships were one-time events — such as guest speakers, special demonstrations, tours, use of community facilities — and incentives — such as special awards, scholarships, and other incentives for students.

Partnerships with Fortune 500 Companies

In 1990 Kuhn surveyed the Fortune 500 companies to assess the status of their participation in school partnerships. More than 60% of the Fortune 500 and Service 500 companies responded, and all but 2% were engaged in some type of education partnership. Following are key findings:

- 78% of companies contributed money;
- 76% provided summer or part-time employment for students;
- 64% contributed materials or equipment;
- 59% encouraged employees to run for school boards;
- 48% participated in school-community partnership programs;
- 26% offered teachers summer employment;
- 22% lobbied legislatures for reform;
- 18% supported tax increases or bond issues; and
- 12% provided executives-on-loan to schools.

The focus on monetary and in-kind contributions outweighed the human resources invested by these companies and organizations at that time.

Benefits of Partnerships

Partnerships are designed so that everyone benefits. Some of the ways that each of the participants might benefit are identified in the following statements.

Students:
- Become better-informed consumers.
- Are exposed to additional positive role models.
- Learn about career choices.
- Take pride in their expanded community, which sometimes results in less vandalism and loitering.
- Discover how classroom learning links to the workplace.
- Develop a heightened motivation for learning.
- Can acquire a better self-image and self-confidence.
- Develop a more positive attitude about their community.
- Become more involved in their community.

Educators:
- Become better informed about expectations of their students in the workplace.
- Receive support and recognition for their expertise.
- Gain expertise to aid in the compatibility of instruction with workplace needs.
- Gain team members who assist in the teaching of students.
- Become more aware of resources and available support.
- Gain a better understanding of the business world and community.

Business employees and organization members:
- Receive better-trained, future employees.
- Contribute to the development of the community and human resources.
- Make a real difference for kids.

- Enhance their community relations efforts.
- Receive recognition for their efforts in the schools.
- Become more attached to their organization, which may result in retention of good employees.
- Acquire a better understanding of societal needs.
- Understand the education system and its complexities.

Communities:
- Have a better school system because of active citizen participation.
- Provide a better quality of life for youth and adults.
- Attract new business and residents to whom education is important.
- Provide a healthier economic environment.
- Gain a better understanding between the taxpayers and schools.
- Have reduced long-term social service expenses by promoting intervention and becoming involved.
- Have a more employable future workforce.
- Have a more connected community.

30 Partnership Projects

In 1986, Otterbourg surveyed more than 100 partnership programs. At that time, Adopt-a-School was the most common type of program, with volunteer programs the second most numerous. Other organizational models, in order of frequency from most to least common, were: school, business, university, civic organization alliances; community schools; foundations; clearinghouses; county-wide projects; committees; regional associations; statewide organizations; and other miscellaneous structures, such as magnet schools and lobbying groups.

It is relatively easy to illustrate some of these types of partnerships. The following list includes some of the pioneering efforts in Lincoln, Nebraska:

1. A high school class is co-taught by researchers from Harris Laboratories and a teacher from Lincoln High School. Students are linked with a mentor from the business to complete their research project and are hooked up via the Internet.

2. Davis Design Company organizes architects and experts in the field to work with design teams from every senior high to develop and present an actual community project. A jury of architects responds to the presentations.

3. Bryan Memorial Hospital is a training site for 18- to 21-year-old, special-needs, transition students, assisting them in developing job skills while providing excellent support for the hospital.

4. McDonald's Restaurant employees and classroom educators developed hands-on mathematics stations relating to the workplace. Educators trained McDonald's employees to assist them in their teaching of these sessions that meet grade-level curriculum objectives. Employees from McDonald's teach these lessons to every student in grade school — each at the developmentally appropriate level — through hands-on activities.

5. Burger King Restaurant organized student leadership seminars with key community leaders where they interacted in small groups. Each school team followed up with planning a leadership activity at their own school.

6. State Farm Insurance Companies provided tutors on site for students from the middle school with the help of Lincoln Action Program, which bused the students to the work site after school.

7. Companies expanding into other countries used foreign-language teachers' expertise to translate manuals and teach executives about the culture of the foreign land.

8. Students and school staff introduced various companies' employees to the Internet.

9. Business personnel and community members served on interview teams when hiring new school administrators.

10. A coalition of 11 schools and their partners worked together to promote family literacy through special events, incentive programs, and media promotions. Each partnership identified a way to assist with this shared goal.

11. Business sites were used for classroom learning, job shadowing, and mentoring.

12. Groups with an interest in promoting math, science, engineering, and technology interests cooperated to provide experts in the field to teach enhanced hands-on lessons, provided by experts in the field, to every seventh-grader in the school system.

13. The American Red Cross recruited volunteers from companies with an interest in health and safety to provide Basic Aid Training, which met a curriculum objective, to every fourth-grade student (2,400) in the school system. School nurses provided the introductory lessons at the schools and the follow-up activities

after the training. Classes were taught at Southeast Community College in two days over spring break.

14. T.O. Haas, a local tire store owner, planted a garden with local school children from Lakeview Elementary, which helped them understand plant life, provided food to eat, and served as a daily checkpoint for students in the summer months.

15. The Architectural Partnership, Nebraska Nurseries, and Maxey School worked with students to plan, implement, and nurture their outdoor classroom.

16. Students ran a re-use center for schools, where businesses donated everything from crayons to computers.

17. The Gallup Organization helped classroom educators to identify their strengths and helped them learn how to capitalize on them.

18. Student artwork and poetry were highlighted in the yellow pages of Aliant Communications' phone book. Student art also was framed by A&R Fine Arts and Framing and put on a year-long rotation in local business sites.

19. Partnership businesses provided Junior Achievement instruction for all elementary students in their partnership school.

20. Students at Sheridan Elementary School wrote and produced a monthly television show with the help of experts and the use of the facilities at CableVision-Time Warner.

21. Public service announcements that promote public education and partnerships were on four local radio stations weekly and on the cable television stations through special partnership efforts.

22. University of Nebraska football players served as mentors to more than 20 high-needs, middle school students in what was called the "Teammates" program. Football coach Dr. Tom Osborne and his wife, Nancy, met with the students and their mentors monthly. Workshops on goal setting, financial investing, applying for a job, and others, were arranged. The middle school students were supported throughout their high school years. Tom and Nancy Osborne provided postsecondary education funding for each of the "Teammates." Summer camp opportunities and other benefits were also provided to these students.

23. Nebraska Wesleyan University students and staff volunteered more than 900 hours a semester at Huntington Elementary School. Elementary students were encouraged to attend events on campus, such as art shows, drama performances, and sporting events, with their families. Foreign language clubs were provided for interested elementary students, taught by the college students. College students found something that felt a lot like home through this relationship. The partnership also was valuable to college students as they gained valuable experience, added credible skills to their résumés, and gained insight into their own careers. Many of the sporting teams provided "reading buddies" for students in need.

24. Commercial Federal developed a banking curriculum with the help and guidance of classroom educators. Classroom instruction was provided by company employees.

25. Valentino's, an Italian restaurant, provided "High Five" awards for exemplary patterns of effort. Each ed-

ucator had access to these awards. This program was designed with administrators and educators. Elementary students get an award in the shape of a hand, a "High Five." Sixteen students, selected at random, received a $500 savings bond and were recognized at a large banquet. All students who received a "High Five" were recognized by name in a newspaper insert.

26. Third-graders had a primary objective of learning about "communities." To aid in their understanding, they had a historical tour of the downtown and rode the Star Tran bus to the area. They learned how to read maps and schedules to meet other objectives. Woods Brothers real estate agents accompanied the students and brought ponchos for each student to aid in safety and easy identification. Agent's cellular phones provided the necessary communication to enhance safety and communication.

27. KFOR radio station provided the leadership and recruited additional business/volunteer support for Student Vote activities for major elections.

28. Smith Barney Inc. provided awards for youths who did community service. Categories were established for different grade levels. Each student who volunteered the designated number of hours was honored at a celebration during National Volunteer Week and highlighted in a newspaper advertisement.

29. Student post offices were set up in elementary schools through the U.S. Postal Service's "Wee Deliver" program.

30. Substitute time was made available to educators who wished to spend a day in industry. Course credit

was given to educators who outlined a curriculum objective and spent summer hours with a business to complete that objective.

Partnership Program Locations

In 1991 the National Association of Partners in Education (NAPE) conducted a survey identifying the location of partnership programs. Forty-eight percent of the respondents involved in partnerships functioned in urban areas, compared to 23% in suburban areas and 5% in rural areas. The major purposes of these partnerships were student services (49%), establishing districtwide policies to address reform issues (27%), and assisting with curriculum development and classroom instruction (24%).

An additional study later in 1991 was completed by NAPE. A random sample of 1,532 school districts was sorted by size of district — urban, suburban, and rural. This study identified that smaller businesses of fewer than 50 employees were the most frequent partner in urban districts. Urban districts also had the greatest number of partnerships, and suburban areas had the greatest number of individual volunteers. Suburban partnerships donated more money to schools, and parent volunteers were the most frequent partners in suburban and rural school districts (NAPE 1992).

Small businesses clearly took a more active role in urban schools, and parent volunteers were prevalent in suburban and rural school districts. With parents included in the figures, more than 2.5 million volunteers were identified. Overall, 65% of the public schools in America were estimated to have partnerships.

In reference to Mann's four hallmarks, the NAPE study did not distinguish between "new" partnerships and the older, more traditional arrangements. One new hallmark was identified — which partnerships had identified leaders. In the NAPE study of 1991, 70% of the urban programs, 34% of the suburban areas, and 30% of the rural areas had an identified director. In this study the finding for types of partnership programs had changed: 33% curriculum and instruction, 31% direct student support, 22% districtwide policy, and 14% professional development.

In a study by Hopkins (1995), basic information about demographics of partnership directors was identified for the first time, and organizational management of partnerships was analyzed for its relationship to program success. In the Hopkins study 40% of the partnership programs existed in urban areas, 16% in suburban areas, 15% in county systems or regions with a population of over 50,000, 15% in rural areas, and 14% in county systems with a population under 50,000 people. Nearly half of the partnership programs (46%) involved all of the schools in a given demographic area.

Respondents also were asked when their partnership program began. Program operation periods ranged from several months to 30 years. Most programs had been in operation for seven years, which would have been since 1987, or four years after President Reagan established the Private Sector Initiatives program.

The funding sources for partnership program staff and activities, according to the Hopkins study, fell into three categories: collaboratively funded (54%, school and community funding); school-based (36%, funded by schools only); and community-based (10%, no school funding). Funding relationships had changed as partnerships took on new forms. Eleven years earlier, in 1984, schools were the primary funding agency for such programs.

The Hopkins study also found that 58% of the partnership directors viewed the funding for the program and staff as secure for one to three years, 11% viewed funding as secure for four to six years, and 31% viewed funding as secure for a period of seven years or more.

Partnership Organization

Two patterns emerged for partnership organization: affiliation with a school administrative unit or department and reporting to a top or middle-level manager.

Affiliation with a school administrative unit or department. In the Hopkins study, partnership directors were asked to identify the administrative unit or department with which they were most closely affiliated in the school system. Table 1 shows the results. More than one-third of the directors worked most closely with the superintendent's office. Nearly one-fourth were closely connected to the public relations or community relations office. In successful partnership programs, the

directors had a direct tie to the superintendent, even
they did not report directly to that individual. That
access provided a way to cut through bureaucratic bar-
riers that sometimes turned volunteers and agencies
away from partnerships.

Table 1. Affiliation of partnership program directors.

Affiliation	Percentage
Superintendent's Office	38
Public/Community Relations	24
Curriculum/Instruction	12
Vocational Education	11
Guidance/Counseling	6
Human Resources/Personnel	3
Office of Grants	3
State/Federal Programs	3

Reporting to top or middle managers. According to this
study, 62% of the partnership directors reported to top-
level managers. The other 38% reported to middle-level
managers. But again, the real key to success was that
directors had direct ties to the school superintendents,
regardless to whom they reported directly.

Board Representation and Coalitions

Successful partnerships build broad coalitions of community support through representation by diverse
groups of stakeholders on a partnership governing board
or advisory council. Table 2 shows the stakeholder
groups identified as being on the decision-making boards
of partnership programs according the percentage of programs with such representation (Hopkins 1995).

Table 2. Board representation.

Stakeholder Group	Percentage of Programs
School Administrators	88
Business Representatives	84
Teachers	71
Superintendents	68
Chamber of Commerce Representatives	53
Community Group Representatives	50
Parents	50
Assistant Superintendents	42
Students	35
Parent Organization Representatives	32
Government Employees	26
Teacher Union Representatives	23
Professional Trade Organizations	23
Cultural Agencies	16
Junior League	9

For those partnership program directors who paid attention to modern management practices, the boards became a coalition of support. Partnership programs that had a broad community and grassroots base on their board achieved a higher level of program success.

Staffing Partnerships

Mann (1984*a*) found that only one-fourth of large urban districts had partnership directors, or some individual identified to manage a partnership program. He identified that factor to be a hallmark of the new wave of cooperation and participation with schools. In the Hopkins study, only 1,875 partnership directors could be identified through at least eight different avenues. Of those directors, 61% were full-time directors; 39%

were identified as part-time directors. Volunteers served as the program coordinators for 7% of the programs. Secretaries served full time in 54% of the programs and part time in 46%; and volunteer secretaries served in 3% of the partnership programs. Only 26% of the directors indicated that they spent 100% of their time on partnerships.

Characteristics of Partnership Directors. Partnership directors were a rarity in 1983 when this new movement began. As they have come on board, a variety of models of structure and influence has evolved. They have created their positions from ground zero and developed the position into one of influence, with a direct relationship with the superintendent of schools. Today partnership directors, with the role of community organizer, come from varied backgrounds and are highly educated. They have learned the fine art of balancing the interests of business, education, parents, the community, and students.

The norm for partnership directors is 15 years of experience in education, according to Hopkins, including an additional four years in the for-profit world and four years in human services, as well as at least 10 years as a volunteer. This varied background explains how successful partnership directors identify with people in both private and public sectors and function well with a large group of volunteers.

Most partnership directors bring a wealth of education training to their positions. Twelve percent of the directors held a doctorate degree; 39% had additional credits beyond a masters degree; and 17% had a masters degree. In sum, 68% of the partnership directors had a minimum of a masters degree.

Salary. The annual salary range for partnership directors in 1994 was $40,000 to $60,000. For men the range was $50,000 to $60,000; for women the range was $40,000 to $50,000. The difference between the salaries for men and women was significant. But the reason for the difference was not easily identifiable. Three out of every four partnership directors were women.

Although the partnership director was identified as a key person in the leadership of partnerships, principals, chief executive officers (CEOs), school liaisons, and business liaisons also provide vital roles.

Job Description. The partnership director usually assists in matching needs and resources through the partnership process and in monitoring program success and providing training to enhance partnerships. The partnership director's responsibilities often include:

- Identifying the overall goals for the partnership program;
- Working with the board of directors or a partnership steering committee;
- Keeping stakeholders informed and involved;
- Monitoring the balance of active participation of all stakeholders;
- Communicating the goals and objectives of the program;
- Recruiting new partners, based on needs;

- Helping schools and businesses identify their needs and resources;
- Establishing partnership policies;
- Coordinating districtwide and partnership program-wide needs;
- Networking with other agencies with common goals;
- Promoting the success stories;
- Researching models of excellence; and
- Keeping records of activities and trends.

Roles of the Principal and the CEO

The school principal and CEO of a business or community organization provide a vital link for communication and support for partnership programs. Each should work with his or her staff members to identify a liaison to work with the partnership program and provide leadership to it. Key duties of principals and CEOs include:

- Setting a positive tone for the partnership activities;
- Being visible at school-community partnership events and districtwide partnership events;
- Facilitating opportunities for the liaison to communicate with a larger audience to recruit volunteers and identify needs;
- Communicating organizational guidelines that the liaison must follow; and
- Supporting and providing leadership for the identification of needs and resources for partnership activities.

Similarly, the school and community-business liaisons should work as a team to develop, nurture, and support partnership activities. Key responsibilities of these individuals include:

- Developing a strong, professional relationship with the partnership liaison;
- Matching needs with resources;
- Planning projects with the partnership council;
- Sharing information with other staff and parents;
- Developing specific objectives for partnership activities;
- Assisting in identification of needs and goals;
- Promoting activities with administrators, executives, colleagues, parents, students, and the media;
- Identifying key personnel to work on the partnership council team (joint committee of the partnering organizations);
- Recruiting, motivating, and recognizing volunteers;
- Maintaining a record of volunteers and activities;
- Obtaining support from immediate supervisors for release of employees;
- Evaluating activities with participants;
- Reviewing the effectiveness of activities and making modifications as needed; and
- Communicating with the partnership director.

Finally, a partnership council should include representatives of all of the stakeholders. Special attention should be paid to the coalitions that can be built with business personnel, key organizations, school administrators, teachers, civic organizations, parents, and students.

Representatives of key groups can enable the partnership council to further network with organizations. Effective partnership councils have the following responsibilities:

- Promoting partnership activities in their organizations and in the community;
- Providing a shared vision and mission;
- Bringing additional resources to the leadership of the program;
- Sharing and supporting the work of the partnership director;
- Providing committee leadership to joint subcommittees that involve additional volunteer leadership;
- Ensuring that all stakeholders are part of the partnership council or have some direct link to decision making; and
- Coordinating multiple partnerships.

A few words about this last item: As partnership programs continue to grow, develop, and evolve, schools have made partners with multiple businesses or organizations. Some organizations also have more than one school or program as partners. There are several models for development and utilization of multiple partners:

One Partnership Council with Multiple Partners. In this model, one partnership council coordinates the efforts of multiple partners through monthly meetings with their partnership schools. This team approach promotes interdisciplinary learning. Some activities may focus on just the expertise of individual businesses. Other projects involve all partners. In this model, the schools' partners also become partners with each other. Meeting on a regular basis is extremely important!

Curriculum Department Organization Model. In a secondary model program where curriculum departments are the organizational model of instruction, partnerships might be made according to instructional departments where the expertise or interest of the community entity matches the curriculum objectives.

Grade Level/Team Organizational Model. At the elementary or middle school level, where the instructional team approach is used, student experiences or curriculum-related activities might best be explored through partnerships with grade levels or teams.

Districtwide Model. Many partnerships develop a specific focus that they wish to share with every student in a curriculum department or grade level. In this model, educators work closely with the community agency or business to assist in the development of the programs to be delivered to the students. Although organizations may dream of this model, they must understand the magnitude of the number of students at each grade level in the district or in the district curriculum department.

Coalition-Based Model. In this model, multiple businesses, agencies, and organizations are invited to the table with classroom educators, curriculum consultants, and district administrators to plan a specific project to reach a multitude of students in order to meet a specific need. Plenty of planning time is needed to allow for the coalition to be built, coordinated, and organized. Subcommittees frequently are organized to handle the many aspects of a huge project that might be approached by a coalition of partners and educators.

Support and Success

State, regional, and national support for partnerships has evolved. In 1995 at least 33 states were state affiliates with the National Association of Partners in Education. Forty-five percent of the partnership directors said there was someone in their respective state education agency to work on partnership efforts. Several states had legislated mandates to continue to support partnership programs.

The National Association of Partners in Education also has developed a 12-step approach to partnership programs. A few of the most important steps are as follows:

Mission. Stakeholders should identify the mission for their partnership program and projects — together. That mission should be widely communicated and easily understood. The primary mission of school-community partnerships must include and focus on student needs.

Matching Needs and Resources. Partnerships are about relationships, and schools are about helping students learn. Partnerships should develop to enhance student learning by having educators, parents, community members, and business representatives working together. Human resources are more important than monetary resources. Focusing only on donated dollars puts partnerships at risk.

Mutual Benefits. Partnerships are successful only when they are mutually beneficial. School personnel have a great deal to offer. School personnel frequently are well-versed in multicultural awareness; dealing with drug and alcohol identification, prevention, and intervention; teaching techniques; public speaking skills; computer literacy; and basic skills instruction. These are valued assets in many businesses and community agencies. Similarly, use of school facilities provides many businesses and community groups with a welcome expansion of space for training meetings and activities. The partners may become even more of a team if they work on wellness programs together using the school facilities.

Communication and Community Relations. Keeping all of the stakeholders informed is a must. Stakeholders include classroom educators, teachers unions, school personnel, school administrators, central office administrators, business personnel, chief executive officers, taxpayers, students, parents, parent organizations, civic organizations, and community members. Business and community partners also benefit from good community relations. Involvement with the schools enhances their public image. Promoting partnership activities can take on several faces. Nearly every business or organization has some sort of newsletter, as do schools. Promoting partnership activities through stories in the company and school newsletters is a great means of sharing the story of what partners are doing together.

Leadership. A partnership director should be identified, whether that position is an addition to a current job role or becomes a separate position. The amount of time a director spends on partnerships usually depends on the number of students being served through the program and the size of the school district. Partnership directors must present a balanced approach to the interests of all of the stakeholders. Business personnel, community members, classroom educators, parents, and students must all feel well represented by directors of these programs. The directors are the link to each group of stakeholders.

Commitment. Top leaders in the private sector, public sector, and schools must be committed to partnerships to ensure success. The partnership director should have direct access to the superintendent of schools and to other major decision makers in each key organization sponsoring the partnership program.

Recognition. Volunteers make the difference, and so steps must be taken to recognize individuals who volunteer and the companies that support them. Key leaders in the schools and community deserve recognition for excellence. Recognition also reinforces partners who are shining examples of excellence, modeling what should and could be done.

Evaluation. Each program should be evaluated by the people involved. Such evaluations are useful only if the results are reviewed and changes are made for improvements based on the results. Results need to be shared. Individual partnership projects, as well as the overall partnership program, need to be evaluated on a consistent basis. Management techniques need to be assessed. Procedures and policies need to change with the times, and practice should be consistent with policies.

In summary, school-community partnerships provide a powerful source of support for schools. They help us build strong communities by working together. By paying attention to good practice and by using "common sense," partnership programs can be extremely successful.

When the public is once again actively engaged in public education, it will make a difference. The indicators of partnership program success provide the "commonsense" checklist of how best to work together.

Significant growth of partnership programs has occurred in the United States. The National Association of Partners in Education is providing leadership and assisting with the development of state organizations.

Because of the difference in how partnerships are defined, regardless of whether they include the traditional parent involvement and career education programs, exactly identifying the number of programs across the United States is difficult. But a clear trend is the development of new programs that exhibit Mann's four hallmarks:

- a coordinating structure,
- multiple purposes,
- multiple players, and
- stability.

The need for partnership programs continues to grow. School "connectedness" with the community and businesses is needed to help public schools remain vital in our changing world.

Resources

Adams, D. "Effective School Business Partnerships." *School Business Affairs* 51 (January 1985): 18-19, 50.

Adams, D., and Snodgrass, P., ed. *A Manager's Handbook to Partnerships*. Ellenton, Fla.: InfoMedia, 1990.

Asche, J. *Handbook for Principals and Teachers*. Alexandria, Va.: National Association of Partners in Education, 1989.

Association for Supervision and Curriculum Development. "Guidelines for Business Involvement in Schools." *Educational Leadership* 47, no. 4 (1990): 84-86.

Burke, M. "School Business Partnerships: Trojan Horse or Manna from Heaven?" *NASSP Bulletin* 70, no. 93 (1986): 45-46, 48-49.

Business Roundtable. *The Role of Business in Education Reform: Blueprint for Action*. Report of the Business Roundtable Ad Hoc Committee on Education. New York, 1988.

Caton, J., and Krchniak, S. "What Makes School-Business Partnerships Successful?" *Business Education Forum* 45, no. 8 (1991): 3-6.

Decker, L., and Romney, V., ed. *Educational Restructuring and the Community Education Process*. Charlottesville: University of Virginia, 1992.

Erickson, M.R., and Kochhar, C.A. *Business Education Partnerships for the 21st Century*. Gaithersburg, Md.: Aspen, 1993.

Globe, T. *Synthesis of Existing Knowledge and Practice in the Field of Educational Partnerships*. Springfield, Va.: U.S. Department of Education, 1990. Eric Document No. 325-535.

Hopkins, B. "School-Community Partnership Structures and Program Success." Ann Arbor: University of Michigan, 1995. Eric Document No. 9538620.

Hyland, T. "Avoiding the Dark Side of School-Business Partnerships." *NASSP Bulletin* 72, no. 512 (1988): 107-109.

Information Technology Foundation. *Roadmap to Success 2000*. Arlington, Va., 1993.

Johnson, J. "The Private Sector Should Help U.S. Schools." *Financier* 15, no. 9 (September 1991): 34-36.

Kuhn, S.E. "How Business Helps Schools." *Fortune* 122, no. 12 (Spring 1990): 91-94.

Levine, M. "Business and the Public Schools." *Educational Leadership* 43, no. 50 (1986): 47-48.

Levine, M., and Trachtman, R. *American Business and the Public Schools: Case Studies of Corporate Involvement in Public Education*. New York: New York Committee for Economic Development, 1988.

Mann, D. "It's Up to You to Steer Those School/Business Partnerships." *American School Board Journal* 171, no. 10 (1984): 20-24. a

Mann, D. "With the Superintendent in the Driver's Seat, the Board Can Map the Route." *American School Board Journal* 171, no. 10 (1984): 23-28. b

Mann, D. "Business Involvement and Public School Improvement, Part 1." *Phi Delta Kappan* 69 (October 1987): 123-28. a

Mann, D. "Business Involvement and Public School Improvement, Part 2." *Phi Delta Kappan* 69 (November 1987): 228-32. b

McDonald, A. "Solving Educational Problems Through Partnerships." *Phi Delta Kappan* 68 (June 1986): 752-53.

McDonald, N. *Criteria Standards & Indicators: Business Educa-tion Partnerships Assessment Tool*. Alexandria, Va.: National Association of Partners in Education, 1993.

Meadows, B. "Nurturing Cooperation and Responsibility in a School Community." *Phi Delta Kappan* 73 (February 1992): 480-81.

Merenda, D. *A Practical Guide to Creating and Managing School/Community Partnerships*. Alexandria, Va.: National Association of Partners in Education, 1986.

Molnar, A.; Merenda, D.; Anderson, D.; and Ubois, M. "Guidelines for Business Involvement in Schools." *Educa-tional Leadership* 57, no. 4 (1990): 68-69.

National Alliance for Business. *The Compact Project: School-Business Partnerships for Improving Education*. Washington, D.C. ERIC Document Reproduction No. ED 312 487.

National Association of Partners in Education. *Business & Education: A Practical Guide to Creating and Managing a Bus-iness/Education Partnership*. Alexandria, Va., 1989.

National Association of Partners in Education. *National School District Partnerships Survey*. Washington, D.C.: U.S. De-partment of Education, 1991.

National Association of Partners in Education. *Partnerships: A Call for Change*. White Paper. Alexandria, Va., 1992.

National Center for Education Statistics. *Education Partner-ship in Public Elementary and Secondary Schools, 1987-1988*. OERI Publication No. CS 89-060. Washington, D.C.: U.S. Government Printing Office, 1989.

National Education Association. *Bring Business and Commun-ity Resources into Your Classroom*. Washington, D.C., 1991.

National PTA and Chrysler Corporation. *Education in Amer-ica: Getting the Nation Involved*. New York: Newsweek, 1991.

O'Connell, C. *How to Start a School/Business Partnership*. Fast-back 226. Bloomington, Ind.: Phi Delta Kappa Educational Foundation, 1985.

Office of Educational Research and Improvement. *An Overview of Evaluation Research on Selected Educational Partnerships*. Washington, D.C., 1991.

Otterbourg, S. *School Partnerships Handbook: How to Set Up and Administer Programs with Business, Government and Your Community*. Englewood Cliffs, N.J.: Prentice-Hall, 1986.

Otterbourg, S. *How to Monitor and Evaluate Partnerships in Education: Measuring Their Success*. Ellenton, Fla.: Info-Media, 1990.

Page, E.G. "Partnerships: Making a Difference over Time?" *Journal of Career Development* 13, no. 3 (1987): 43-49.

Perry, N. "Saving the Schools: How Business Can Help." *Fortune Special Report* (November 1988): 42-56.

Purcell, E. *Partners for the 80s: Business and Education*. Alexandria, Va.: National School Volunteer Program, 1981.

Rist, M. "Mass Marketers Have a Sweet Deal for You, But There Are Strings Attached." *American School Board Journal* 176, no. 9 (1990): 20-24, 39.

Rist, M. "Angling for Influence." *American School Board Journal* 177, no. 4 (1990): 20-25.

Ruffin, S., Jr. "School-Business Partnerships: Laying the Foundation for Successful Programs." *School Business Affairs* 50, no. 2 (1984): 14-15, 38-40.

Seeley, D.S. "Educational Partnership and the Dilemmas of School Reform." *Phi Delta Kappan* 65 (February 1984): 383-85.

Trachtman, R. "School-Business Collaborations: A Study of the Process and Product." Doctoral dissertation, Hofstra University, 1985.

U.S. Department of Education. *America 2000: Strategies for Reform*. Washington, D.C.: U.S. Government Printing Office, 1991.

Woodside, W. "Business in Education: Is There Life After Partnerships?" *NASSP Bulletin* 70, no. 490 (1986): 6-11.

National Partnership Organizations

For additional information on school-community-business partnerships, contact the following organizations:

National Association of Partners in Education
901 North Pitt Street, Suite 320
Alexandria, VA 22314
Phone: (703) 836-4880
Fax: (703) 836-6941
E-mail: NAPEHQ@aol.com

Partnership Directors Network
P.O. Box 21894
Lincoln, NE 68542-1894
Phone: (402) 436-1990
Fax: (402) 436-1620
E-mail: bhopkins@lps.esu18.k12.ne.us